I0560325

Unrealized Reality

A Mental Health Story

Dedication

To my husband, whose motivational support, enthusiasm for my personal growth, and unwavering love have been the foundation of my journey. Your belief in me, even in moments when I doubted myself, has given me the strength to pursue my dreams and share my story unapologetically—a pursuit to face reality in the security of unconditional love.

To my kids, Tré and Zoë, who are too young now, but will one day understand that mommy's journey was the motivator to approach motherhood fearlessly and embrace every challenge as an opportunity for growth.

To my friends, my soulmates, who have been my pillars of support, laughter, and inspiration; your unwavering belief in me has made this journey possible. You are the family that I have chosen with all my heart.

To all my guardian angels, who accompanied me on my life's journey and graciously offered parental love and guidance I didn't know I needed. Your unabating support and protection have shielded me through times of uncertainty, and for that, I am eternally grateful.

And to anyone who dares to embrace their story – may you find the courage to voice your truth and inspire others in the process. This memoir is for you.

Unrealized Reality

TABLE OF CONTENTS

"There have been so many people who have said to me, 'You can't do that,' but I've had an innate belief that they were wrong. Be unwavering and relentless in your approach."

—*Halle Berry*

INTRODUCTION

Much like Dorothy in the Wizard of Oz, my journey began with a storm — unsettling revelation that what I had been told, particularly about my father and the early days of my life, was nothing more than a carefully woven fabric of lies. The wizard, in my case, was a deceptive narrative that had shaped the very foundation of my existence. The curtain had been drawn back, or more accurately, ripped apart, exposing a truth far removed from the terrible stories I had grown up accepting as reality.

With the realization that the pillars of my family's history were built on falsehoods, I found myself catapulted into a yearlong quest for the truth, akin to Dorothy's quest to find her way back home. The yellow brick road of my own discovery led me through the twists and turns of buried secrets, dysfunctional family dynamics, and the strange events that had constructed the facade I had known for decades. The shocking truth became a catalyst for a profound identity crisis, urging me to peel back the layers of deception that had concealed my true heritage.

We like to believe that there is always a happy ending — a proverbial happily ever after like some vapid sitcom where everything works out in the end. Sorry to break it to you, but life doesn't really work that way. In fact, it usually doesn't.

Sometimes truth is stranger than fiction. Sometimes broken things can't be fixed. And sometimes, you have to create your own happily ever after.

In the quiet corners of my memory, I continue to do the difficult work of reconciling my history — a story that unfolds like the pages of a worn-out book—tattered and torn filled with memories and revelations etched with the raw strokes of reality. Like it or not, mine is a story that speaks of brokenness and the fragments of what once was.

I repeat, sometimes broken things can't be fixed. Sometimes the distance between you and someone you love widens, hollowing out a silent canyon between you that echoes with the weight of grievances, betrayals, and mysteries unsolved. It was a bitter truth to swallow—the acknowledgment that sometimes, despite our most fervent efforts, relationships are irreparable so long as people fail to fix the brokenness in themselves.

The good news, though, is that from the broken pieces, we can create something new and, perhaps, even better than what existed. Nowhere is this better demonstrated than in the age-old art of Kintsugi, a Japanese practice that celebrates the beauty of imperfection. In Kintsugi, broken pottery is not discarded. Never that. Instead, it is meticulously pieced back together with lacquer, carefully gluing back the pieces. Not every piece, however, fits perfectly, as it's too shattered to be returned to the pot. The result is a pot with cracks, gaps, and holes. But, in their wisdom, Kintsugi masters mix together a liquid comprised of powdered gold, silver, and platinum. This liquid is carefully poured into the broken places. The result is a mosaic of gold veins, turning the shattered vessel into a wonder of resilience and beauty far lovelier than the old clay pot it once was and stronger than it ever had been. Life has taught me that, just like Kintsugi, from the remnants of our broken pieces, we can create something extraordinary. It's a life skill that requires patience and acceptance, acknowledging the fractures without denying their existence, but at the same time, not being defined by them. The scars become part of the narrative, not a blemish to be hidden, but a testament to endurance and the capacity to transform pain into something beautiful.

It was a long and difficult road to dig up the truth about my family and how I came to be. In the chapters of my family's story, I sought to find the metaphorical gold. It was a delicate dance between acknowledging the past and forging a new narrative for the future. But, with my amazing husband by my side, we made the phone calls, traveled to the places of the past, and reconstructed the story to get to the truth. Perhaps that is how we grew stronger, individually and as a couple. What remains is the promise of new connections and a future without the toxicity that created the lies in the first place.

In spite of all that happened and all that continues to happen, a stark reality remains: my family has played a role in shaping the strength and beauty that is seen in my life now. I am who I am because they are who they are. Their legacy, whether a source of inspiration or a challenge to overcome, is an indelible mark on the canvas of my journey.

I have, I'm sure, inherited some of their good traits — lessons in kindness, moments of shared joy, and the resilience to weather life's storms. But I have also been shaped by learning to survive the trauma, by navigating the shards of broken connections and emerging with a mosaic of scars that tell a story of both pain and triumph. It's a duality that makes me resilient, compassionate, and, in many ways, a reflection of the Kintsugi artistry that has transformed my familial fractures into a unique and enduring work of art.

I have become the woman I am today because of them or in spite of them, a dichotomy that defines the complex dance between nature and nurture. In the crucible of our shared history, I've learned lessons not just in joy and love but also in resilience and the art of forging strength from fragments.

It takes great courage to look at your life without the benefit of rose-colored glasses. You just see yourself, your family, and everything around you raw and real. That is what I chose to do. And I was rewarded with a string of aha moments that changed everything. Choosing to see oneself, family, and the world without the distortion of illusion is an arduous journey, one that I willingly embarked upon. The unvarnished truth, though initially daunting, became the lens through which I now see myself and possess a deeper understanding of my existence.

Those aha moments cannot be understated. In facing the stark realities, I was able to cut through the fog of deception. Each revelation was a steppingstone, guiding me closer to the truths I would need for the next level of growth in my life. It was a journey marked by pain and wet with many tears, but the cost was worth the transformative process that fundamentally shifted who I was. Adversity became the catalyst for growth, and the crucible of truth refined me into a version of myself that was stronger, better, and more resilient.

In the coming pages, I invite you to accompany me on this incredible journey of self-discovery. Each revelation, every painful epiphany, and the moments of profound clarity are laid bare as I navigate my past, embrace the present, and prepare for the future. As you read my story, my hope is that you find solace and inspiration, your light within darkness, discovering the strength within to gather your own broken pieces and, much like the art of Kintsugi, form them into something uniquely beautiful.

No, not everything can be fixed. But everything can be transformed.

"Your willingness to look at your darkness is what empowers you to change."

—Iyanla Vanzant

1.

The Incident

How do you view life? I've always felt that I view the world differently than most. You learn the true power of individualism along the journey of life. I'm turning the literary muses upside down…I'm starting from the end; Is this way risky, unfamiliar, and or is it really just a sign of things to come? To understand my past, you must first take a glimpse into my present. I had no idea that at 41, I'd be approaching 5 years of marriage with 2 kids under 5 years old. In parallel, I'm finally standing tall after my most tragic life experience…

I find myself in a state of evolution. It's a deliberate effort to embrace change and growth…acknowledging the fluidity of existence as I navigate the intricacies of self-acceptance.

If you hear anyone talking about self-acceptance with a smile on their faces, you'll know they have a long way to go in their life journey. Self-acceptance is akin to being in an all-out war with yourself and coming out alive on the other side. Ever heard a veteran tell a war story while grinning like a Cheshire cat? Hell no. You can hear the tremble in their voices and see the mist in their eyes. The fires of war are etched in their minds and spirit. They still can't believe they survived and are alive to tell the tale.

Self-acceptance has been an emotional battle I have had to fight from the start of my life until the day you started reading these words. But where physical wars ultimately end, emotional ones may continue for a lifetime. Or perhaps one day I will receive the blessed peace where the past is so obscured, its slimy tentacles can't reach me. That day of freedom has not arrived yet, as I still feel the twinges of pain from the past. I still feel the tears rising in my chest and backing up behind my eyes. And sometimes, every now and then, the rivers of sorrow flow out from me about a past that didn't have to be what it was.

At the core of this narrative lies the pivotal presence of a significant character – my mom. In my journey towards healing, unveiling the truth becomes imperative as I strive to liberate myself from the entanglements of the past. Discussing the complexities surrounding my relationship with my mom emerges as a crucial avenue for me to navigate, confront, and ultimately break free from the shackles of yesterday. It's through this exploration and candid conversation about my mom that I embark on a path toward understanding, resolution, and personal liberation.

It took a long time for me to be ready for the truth that you are about to read. I had to be spiritually mature enough to do it without malice, but I also had to do it without pulling any punches. I won't lie about what really happened.

I am delving into a discussion centered on objective facts from documents forever stored within the courthouse – the indisputable events that transpired, devoid of emotional nuances or personal perspectives or opinions. Let's focus solely on the concrete, factual details that constitute an unbiased account of what unfolded.

This is a hangover from the aftermath.

My goals are simple. The first is purely selfish. My freedom resides on the pages of this book. Pouring it out from soul and for your examination is a declaration of my independence from it all.

The second goal, while it may sound cliché, carries an undeniable truth: I yearn to aid in the liberation of others. Although I don't know anyone else in my situation, I feel confident that I'm not alone. Perhaps you've heard such sentiments before and dismissed them as mere rhetoric, doubting the sincerity of the speaker. Yet, having endured the confines of my own mental prison with my mother as the jailer, breaking free compels me to extend my concerns to those ensnared in similar circumstances. The yearning for freedom becomes a potent force, a shared journey that transcends individual boundaries. It is a drug meant not for hoarding, but for sharing, a universal quest to emancipate others from the shackles of their own minds.'

This is how it happened for me.

Early January of 2021 in Huntsville, AL, the air outside was cold and eerie. Eleven months had passed since COVID-19 changed our lives and provided us with our new normal of ordering food to-go from restaurants, going to the grocery store first thing in the morning to avoid the crowds, and wearing those dreaded masks everywhere we went.

I was dying to get back to what life used to be, before COVID, and the vaccine was just recently approved. I proactively signed up for an early vaccination. I wanted to be first in line to get the shot in hopes of keeping myself and my family safe, and hopefully speeding up us getting to the day when we could all be together. As I waited for my appointment to get the jab, while COVID was confining everyone to their homes, my life took another unexpected turn—I discovered I was pregnant.

Despite my plan and my excitement that I would have some protection from the dreaded disease, the COVID landscape was still evolving every day. Still, I had to make a life decision about a new vaccine that had been developed abnormally fast and the health of my unborn child. Should I still get vaccinated now that I'm pregnant? There was no data or evidence so far to suggest that this vaccine was safe for my unborn child. So, I was faced a life-altering decision.

After I had a day or so to think, it was clear to my husband and I that I would not go through with my scheduled vaccination due to my pregnancy. It was also clear that we were going to wait until after 13 weeks to share this pregnancy with friends and family. In January of 2019, I found out I was pregnant and we were so excited that we shared the news with everyone. Unfortunately, at 8 weeks I had a miscarriage; we had to tell everyone the horrible news. I felt so embarrassed. I was embarrassed that I was unable to carry a child when that's the natural goal of most women.

I was embarrassed discussing the details or even the gut-wrenching appointment where I could clearly see there was no heartbeat on the sonogram.

The day I was scheduled to receive my vaccination, my mother called to get all of the details of my experience. My mom, my husband Rob, and I were always three peas in a pod on the phone. My mom and I talked on the phone everyday regardless of the vaccination, but today was much more interesting. I really didn't want to tell my mom the reason I skipped the vaccination appointment, especially since my husband and I decided we would keep this a secret until we were past the unpredictable period of 13 weeks. But I felt guilty keeping things from my mom and I didn't want her to be concerned, so I revealed the pregnancy secret.

"So, did you get vaccinated?" my mom asked.

In my shy, child-like voice, I admitted that I didn't. What!? Why not!?" she exclaimed.

I finally admitted that I wasn't vaccinated because I found out I was pregnant. I shared the exciting story of my pregnancy test; however, I made it very clear that she was the only person who could know.

"So, you're not going to tell your sister?" she asked.

"No, I'm not telling her. We aren't telling anyone until we get past 13 weeks to ensure we don't have a miscarriage again.'

Following the revelation, a strange air lingered in the aftermath. My mother's behavior took an unusual turn for the worse. My mom expressed how upset she was that I didn't want to share with my sister despite trying to convince me otherwise or stressing that we were the "trio" that doesn't keep secrets from each other. I was trying to defend my decision because of the miscarriage from last year and because it was my choice. I was literally in shock because I was having a "me too" conversation with my own mother.

It was my right to share my pregnancy on my own terms and what made sense to me. Besides, I wasn't close with my sister, which my mom was fully aware of. So, I was stunned that she was pressing for me to share against my wishes.

This debate of sharing the news with my sister slowly grew into an argument. Regardless of how much I expressed my feelings of waiting to share the pregnancy, my mom continued to be upset and threatened to tell my sister anyway. My husband and I begged and pleaded with her to follow my wishes, but she was stern in her position and fully determined to share despite how I felt.

In the coming weeks, there were drastic changes in my daily relationship with my mother. The fun, happy-go-lucky person I spoke with every day was no longer present. You know what it's like when you're on the phone with someone and they are making subtle hints to let you know that aren't happy with you. Yet, when you ask what's wrong, they say, "nothing." But clearly <u>something</u> was wrong.

This new version of my mother that I was experiencing was beyond painful to be on the receiving end of. Her demeanor on our daily calls went from being delightfully entertaining to the bane of my existence. Imagine over 15 years of daily conversation, laughter, and trash talking that comes to a screeching halt and I don't fully understand why. When I finally got past 13 weeks, I called my sister to share the good news. Instead of her offering congrats or asking about my well-being, her first response was, "How come you didn't feel comfortable sharing with me?" The lack of enthusiasm in her response revealed that my mom had already told her about the pregnancy. It was a common, pretty comical occurrence that my mom shared news when she shouldn't have, until now.

Could things get worse? Yes, things got worse.

Tensions escalated as my mother expressed anger over my accusation that she purposely informed my sister regardless of my wishes. My mother was inconsolable, as her thoughts were fixed on her own needs and her own anger. Finally, I had let things fester for long enough. My mother had continuously disregarded me and my feelings for the first seven months of my pregnancy, so long that I knew I was going to have to address it against my will. I didn't want to argue with my mother… my best friend; but she didn't leave me a choice. Do I just accept her behavior because she's my mother and my only parent? Or do I set boundaries? Her new behavior was the most painful thing I've ever experienced.

Imagine your mother hating you and not having a grasp of why she felt that strongly or what I did to cause this disdain for me. So, I sent her a text. Who knew that this message would create a stillness and a response that I never saw coming. Especially not after 15 years of daily fun and living life together.

She unraveled. And after I had some intense counseling sessions to discuss this incident, I kept asking,

"How could this happen? Why would my mother just leave my life for us to never speak again? What has happened here?'

Unfortunately, it's much more common in our society for a father to leave his children, but a mother doing this is almost unheard of. I was sure I knew why. But nothing prepared me for what my counselor said.

"I have not met your mother or your sister, so this would have to be confirmed. But this is evidence of undiagnosed mental illness," she explained.

My mother was mentally ill.

"Embrace what makes you unique, even if it makes others uncomfortable. I didn't have to become perfect because I've learned throughout my journey that perfection is the enemy of greatness."

—*Janelle Monae*

2.

The Aftermath

Prompted by my therapist's advice, I penned a note to my mother, articulating the impact of her actions on my well-being. Why did she have a lack of concern for my pregnancy? And truthfully… my mom had her role in contributing to the strained relationship with my sister. So, this note served as a means to communicate the depth of my feelings, an attempt to name the family dynamics as I had experienced them. This curse had to stop now. Through written words, I could express myself openly and honestly — without interruption. My hope was that she would ponder my thoughts and it might lead us to an understanding and reconciliation while drawing clear lines about how we were to interact moving forward. On August 27th, I sent her this text:

"Hey mommy,

I was going to call you back, but the way our relationship has changed is super toxic. For the past ~7 months, when I've gotten off of the phone with you, I've felt like shit. Then to add insult to injury, the so-called issues you have with me are not things I've ever done to you, so I'm always confused. It finally hit me the other day that you constantly speak on behalf of Heaven as if that is the relationship you and I have had. Since at least 2004/2005, you and I have spoken every day on the phone for hours at a time, until I got pregnant this year (17 yrs). I've shared my time, money, travel, helped you apply for jobs, fixed your credit, bought your home, let you hang out with my friends....I've shared my entire life with you, never held back, always been raw, honest, and forthcoming with my success and my shortcomings, yet for some reason you have issues with how I've treated you!

How? Since I chose not to share MY pregnancy until after the high-risk period, you've gone out of your way to show me your unhappy with my decisions and how I want to handle things; trying to force your opinions on me as if I'm a child. Yes, you're my mother, but I'm an adult. And when I didn't do what you wanted, you changed how you loved me. I cannot emotionally handle your methods, lies, and

22

your inability to admit your wrongs. As if I've been this abusive, inconsiderate, bullying person to you. Now, you basically hate everyone that means the world to me, Rob, Naomi, Tasha, as if they are to be held responsible for your actions. From the moment Rob's family knew I was pregnant (after the high-risk period) they've asked every conversation how I'm doing; they told us they'd be down here no matter what when he's born and have made every effort to show how excited they are to be an uncle and grandparents. This whole pregnancy has been like pulling teeth with you and it's not about you or Heaven! It's even more crazy, you call Naomi, lie and talk shit about me to MY friend, and Naomi's wrong for telling me? It never crossed your mind that you were acting inappropriately.

Did you ever think that your actions/commentary put Naomi in an uncomfortable/tough position? Our level of communication had already died down way before she told me anything because of how you've changed your relationship with me...hating Rob, feeling forced to ask about your own grandchild, clearly letting me know you're still unhappy with me. Naomi is the one who encouraged me to talk to you when I had already decided I was separating myself. It's funny because Naomi and Rob are the reason I didn't step back from you after your behavior changed and your love changed for me. Yet your reality is that Naomi is wrong.

When will you take responsibility for your inappropriate behavior? When will you stop speaking to me about Heaven's feelings? And why do you think I'm so stupid that I don't know you two discuss me when I'm not on the phone? Duh....you and I talked shit about how inconsiderate and closed off Heaven has been for over 10 years, why would you be any different about me? My relationship with Heaven has been shit for the first 32 years of my life and you watched. It's not a figment of my imagination or a one-time incident at 10 years old.

Don't you remember having to semi-threaten Heaven so I could move in with her when I left Dallas in 2014 (I was 32yrs old) since I couldn't stay with you because of George's dog? 32 years of a very distant relationship on both sides was never a concern previously, nor is it my fault for why it still doesn't work now. You've watched our relationship be shit for most of my life and now you blame me for it not being fixed. I've asked her repeatedly to share more with me to build trust and she still chooses not to. Heaven is very closed off, never shares her life with either of us, so why is it expected of me to share my personal life just for her to pass judgement? I didn't even know Heaven and Christian were separating until he had already moved back to FL.

How come she is allowed to share her personal life when it's comfortable for her and I'm wrong for doing the same? Even when Heaven was completely wrong for how she treated me about my current job (being unsupportive and speaking as if she has any experience working at a small biotech), but you never held her accountable. I'm no longer taking responsibility for the demise of our families learned bad behaviors. The same relationship you have with your sisters is the same one I have with mine, yet it's my fault. The relationship I have with you has changed because you think you can force me to behave like you and Heaven. You and Heaven always say, "Everything doesn't have to be discussed." Resolutions and explanations never occur in our family. I speak on issues and then I'm left hanging and no path forward. You both are mute on everything!

I've learned healthier ways to have relationships and communication and I'm not going back to our bad, generational behavior of no communication. It kills marriages,

25

friendships and relationships in general. I'm also no longer taking the blame for the demise of my relationship with you or Heaven. If Heaven wants us to be better, we can discuss how we got here, admit our faults and move forward, but I'm not listening to you speaking on her behalf. If you want to be honest, discuss the truth of how we got here, admit your wrong doings without blaming everyone else, I'll be open to it after the baby is here. For now, this relationship with you doesn't work. I need space and peace for a while, which is why I've stopped our conversations. I'm not initiating any counseling or additional conversations at least until the baby gets here, and maybe longer especially if you're not even willing to be honest, change, or admit your faults.

All in all, I have been forced to set boundaries with you because I haven't deserved this treatment, when the focus should have been my pregnancy and you being a grandmother. My focus is on getting this baby here and building a family with my husband. If you want to be here for the birth, you are more than welcome to contact Rob as he will be more than happy to help arrange or provide information on what you need."

My mother was quick to respond:

> *"I fully hear your boundaries loud and clear. I wish you the best of luck with your son."*

This was the last message I received from my mom on the 27th of August 2021. As I read that message over and over to force myself into reality, I stood in my kitchen in a state of disbelief. The anxiety and hesitation that rose in my chest completely took over my chest, my arms, and my tongue, so much that I couldn't allow a response to leave my phone. And to my surprise, a few days later, I received a message from my sister, Heaven, that stated:

> *"Hi, I'm going to see our mother and I'm not sure how long I'll be there. I had to drag it out of mommy but I saw the text message you sent and I feel you have gone overboard with expressing your feelings and trying to get people to communicate. I have truly been staying neutral in yours and Mommy's drama but your text message crossed the line especially in light of her apologizing for talking bad about you, you two discussing the event and working to move forward. I totally get that you needed space but your words were and are extremely hurtful. You feel justified in the way you handle things and I have taken that same stance regarding this situation. I fully recognize the timing of this sucks and I do not*

send this message lightly but at this point it just is what it is and I have to live with that. I truly wish you the absolute best and I hope you have a super healthy and happy baby boy."

After receiving my sister's message, I called her immediately to understand what she had to do with this disagreement with our mother and to get an understanding of what she meant. How did this even involve her? Was she trying to leave my life too?

There was never an air of concern for how our mother had been treating me for the past 7 months or how her actions made me feel. Especially considering that her hatred for me came out of nowhere. There was never a concern to hear my side of the story to try and help reconcile the situation. There was never a moment where I nor my pregnancy mattered to the two people in my life that I thought loved me like my mom had always expressed.

The call ended with being offered crumbs of a relationship with my sister. If I called or texted, she may or may not have responded since I hurt our mother. Her text wished me the best of luck as if she was never going to speak to me again. Still, I had the privilege to call her when my son was born; but she was unsure how she could maintain a relationship with me.

These were crumbs I wasn t willing to accept from anyone. Had I literally just lost the only two family members that I know in this world? Is this real life? Was my message really mean? How could my mom and sister ignore the mean treatment my mom gave me for months and then blame this entire situation on me? Why don't my feelings matter? Why can't I demand to be treated a certain way just like they do? Do I really have to chase my mom and sister for a relationship now? Was I just supposed to accept unfair treatment and bullying just because it was my family? Just because it was my mom?

What could I have done differently? All I could conclude was that I didn't matter. My feelings didn't matter. And my new family didn't matter either. It was a complete punch to the stomach and cut to my heart. It doesn't happen often, but I was speechless. I haven't talked to either of them since.

"The ultimate measure of a man is not where he stands in moments of comfort and convenience, but where he stands at times of challenge and controversy."

—Martin Luther King, Jr.

3.

The Lie

The prevalent conversation of our era often centers around the idea that people may not be who they claim to be. Social media allows us to hide who we really are, filters disguise our appearance, dating sites let us lie and pretend to be better versions of ourselves. The world seems all too ready to build on lies.

But, when those lies are exposed to the light, everything built on them crumbles.

I, too, discovered that much of my childhood narrative about my father — his identity, my own, and the reasons behind his absence since the age of 6 — was built on nothing but a parade of lies.

The story I had been told by my mother for years was that my father abandoned us when I was just a toddler. I believed that he didn't care about me. To deepen the charade, my mother instituted a ritual. Every graduation year, I was told to send an invitation to him through his mother who was said to be the only person who could reach him. But there was never a reply. That was meant to confirm that he wanted nothing to do with me.

In the face of these revelations, I've found myself opting for laughter over tears, a coping mechanism ingrained in the resilience of Black people who are all too familiar with dealing with trauma. However, beneath the surface, the reality of these discoveries remained undeniably heartbreaking.

From school age to college, I never heard a peep from my father. Over the years, I had been told by my mother that graduation invitations and correspondence about other events were sent to my paternal grandmother's home with hopes that they would make it to my dad. I also knew that my father never paid a dime in child support. He was kind of like a gypsy and lived off the grid, so he was easily able to dodge child support laws.

Despite my father's actions, my mother never spoke negative of him. She never called him a deadbeat or inappropriate names. She always kept it classy and brief, that she left him because he wasn't willing to be her partner in life, pulling his financial weight. She gave me vague puzzle pieces of half-truths and let me, with my childlike understanding, fill in the gaps. She explained that my father lost his job when I was an infant and was never motivated again to work since my mom had everything taken care of from the daycare center income. This is why my mother worked the way she did while I was growing up and thank goodness she did. She always made sure we had what we needed.

Well... almost everything we needed. We still needed him. His love, his care, and his attention.

The generational curses were set up for me to believe that my dad was just like most Black fathers. Uncaring, abandoning, unsupportive pigs.

But he was living off the grid. my mother said, and he skirted child support by working under the table. But I would soon find out each one of the stories I was fed for decades — my whole life — were all lies.

"The way to right wrongs
is to turn the light of
truth upon them."

—Ida B. Wells

4.

How Did We Get Here?

I grew up in San Diego, California in the early 80's. There was always great weather, sandy beaches to play on, and plenty of aunts, uncles, and cousins nearby. By the age of 4, I was a typical statistic: an African American child who had a deadbeat father who left my mother high and dry to raise two kids by herself. My dad was nowhere to be found. I asked my mom about why their divorce happened and if and when he was coming back. I can count on one hand the number of times my dad picked us up to spend time with him.

My mom owned a daycare, so several kids from my class at school and within the neighborhood came to our house after school. My sister and I were living the life. My birthday parties would have almost 100 people there to celebrate and we got a chance to experience all the great kid activities in the city like SeaWorld, Knotts Berry Farms, and Balboa Park.

Shortly after my dad walked out, there were men my mom dated, but I was like all kids, and I didn't want to share my mother's time. Being so young, there's no way to understand how a mother could date anyone else besides their father. And of course, there's a certain level of insecurity that I felt when my dad walked out that made me cling to my mother even tighter.

To add insult to injury, my mom remarried when I was in 3rd grade. My underexperienced brain couldn't comprehend anything, but I knew I didn't want to lose sight or memory of my real father, just in case he came back. The ultimate insult was that I was forced to change my last name for this year at school. Who knew at the age of 8 I could feel embarrassment that people would know my parents were unstable and got divorced due to the new last name. I even got myself into trouble because I refused to write my new last name on my assignments or stand in line for the assembly in the correct alphabetic order. Soon thereafter my child wishes were granted and my mom divorced him. Finally, my name went back to my dad's name.

Who knew over the coming years that the changing of my last name wouldn't be as difficult to endure as all of the moves that occurred. No, we weren't a military family. We moved around by choice. We moved from San Diego to Atlanta when I was going into 5th grade so that my mom could attend court reporting school.

I entered a new school and started from scratch on making new friends. I also developed an affinity for stealing. I went from having everything I wanted to having nothing at all and then a serious feeling of guilt for asking for anything at all; so, I took matters into my own hands.

My mom clearly had her ups and downs during my childhood. But she was the epitome of a strong, resilient woman. She would always put her money where her mouth was; she was always willing to do anything to provide for her family, and that's exactly what she did.

My middle school years were the worst! My horrible, embarrassing habit of theft continued up through my undergraduate years. I fully justified stealing and I never went without the stupid desires I had. Stealing and more moves to better our lives, but they were heavy on the emotions.

Then there were the four to five moves that occurred prior to leaving San Diego. We moved from our home to a trailer, then to an apartment in

Chula Vista, then to another apartment in El Cajon. Exhausting right? Then in March of my 8th grade year, we moved to Maryland where I ultimately graduated from high school. After that, there were several moves within the DMV as well including several apartments in Waldorf, a townhome in Mitchellville my junior year, and then to 2 apartments in DC prior to leaving for college. I've moved so much that I could barely keep up with my belongings or my friendships.

Stability. It was something I desperately wanted. And I was determined to get it.

A great deal of
intelligence can be
invested in ignorance
when the need for
illusion is deep.

—Saul Bellow

5.

Sister Struggles

My sister's inclination towards silence created a kind of aura that was nearly impossible for anyone to penetrate. Despite being three years older than me, her penchant for silence persisted as far back as I can remember and up through her high school and college years. She exuded an unsettling mix of insecurity and withdrawal, along with a demeanor that persisted. It wasn't until many years after college that she broke through her shell and showed us who she would ultimately become. When I recall my childhood with my sister, most of my memories are dark and covered in clouds of complete confusion. From as far back as my memory goes, I longed for closeness from my sister or just a small sense that she liked me as a person at all. This longing lasted until I finally realized that this fantasy relationship I dreamt about, was never going to happen.

Few had the patience to withstand her reticent nature, and my husband, like the rest of us, had limited interactions with her. During our time residing in our D.C. apartment building in my teenage years, my sister would come home and pass by us without uttering a word. She refrained from engaging with anyone, maintaining her mysterious quietude.

The main things I'll never forget are the countless scenarios where it was made clear that I was the sister that was never wanted. Any time we had to sit next to each other in a car or on a park bench, if my arm brushed her arm, she would immediately move to get away from me. The only familial hugs I received from her were forced by my mom. Hugs as if there was disease on my skin and I to this day don't understand why I was treated as if I had the plague.

And I really found out that I was in this world alone when my sister stood by and watched a bully almost kick my ass during recess in 3rd grade. I stepped on her Walkman on the playground (yes, this shows my age), and she threatened to beat me up after school. As the crowd of the other students began to build, there stood my sister resting on a friend's shoulders from her class waiting for the show to start. Luckily, my mom showed up to set the girl straight and defend me.

Throughout my life, I tried to navigate this relationship with my sister, but I always felt I was alone in the desire to even have a sibling. As time progressed, it finally dawned on me why my sister didn't particularly like me. My tumultuous relationship from high school with my mother was told to my sister. My sister seemed to be influenced by the negative image my mom had painted of me, especially through my high school years while she was in college. This sealed the deal for my sister and I to never develop a real sibling relationship.

Our little family was innovative, willing to take risks, and going farther in our professional lives than anyone in our extended family. In the same breath, growing up in my family with all of these constant changes also meant a lonely childhood since there was a nonexistent sibling relationship and a relationship with my mother that got worse by the month. I resorted to staying away from home as much as I could to have some peace from daily life with my mom. Survival became my way of living.

All in all, sisterhood wasn't what it was cracked up to be.

"It's only after you've stepped outside your comfort zone that you begin to change, grow, and transform."

— Roy T. Bennett

6.

High School Daze

After moving to Maryland in March of my 8th grade year, my mom promised me that I would be able to attend the same high school for the entire 4 years, and I wouldn't have to be concerned with moving like I did in elementary and middle school. Despite all of the moves, I was always proud of my mom for having a plan. She always instilled in me that all of the moves were for the greater good of the family.

I went to a high school that was newly opened and was very diverse. I played sports every season of the year, which included volleyball, cheerleading for basketball, and softball. I never had the opportunity to participate in sports in my younger years because they were too expensive, so I was fully determined to participate in everything that my heart desired. I ended up being one of the popular sports kids at my high school with more friends than I could count.

My high school friends and I were kicking it and having so much fun. Or were we? As we reveled in what seemed like carefree moments of laughter and camaraderie, the reality was that a somber truth was lying beneath the surface. We were using the partying and alcohol to numb the pain. The scars from our tumultuous upbringings ran deep, casting a shadow over our seemingly carefree teenage years.

The coping mechanism we frequently turned to was drinking — a means to navigate the traumas of our family's and of the past. Looking back, it seemed like we all had traumas we were facing. We talked about it, yes, but mostly we tried to escape it by getting drunk and dancing the night away.

Reflecting on those times, it becomes painfully evident how messed up we truly were. The mind games and manipulations we endured from the people we called family were profoundly distressing. And we were too young to know how to fight back. Faced with such challenges, it felt like we had no other recourse but to resort to substances like alcohol to find some semblance of control in the middle of the chaos that surrounded us.

I even found a boyfriend (Mason) my sophomore year and he was the first person who showed me what true love meant.

He was a Caucasian kid, a year younger than me with two younger siblings and married parents. I remember he lived in this huge house and his mom was super cool. I remember our first date, which was to a Capitals hockey game with his family. His mom called my mom and asked if I was able to spend the night since the event was going to end late on a school night. Okay, yes, she asked if I was allowed to spend the night at my boyfriend's house. To my jaw dropping surprise, my mom agreed and I spent the night at my boyfriend's house. Holy sh t! I thought I was so grown. Throughout this two-and-a-half-year relationship, we spent an infinite amount of time together and there were countless times I spent the night at his house for various reasons. I had someone who loved everything about me from my head to my toes. I spent so much time with him and his family that his two siblings and mother became like family to me.

Strangely, at the end of my junior year and heading into senior year my spending the night in various situations turned into staying with my boyfriend's family every night. I ate dinner with them, I rode to and from school with my boyfriend, we went to parties on the weekend etc. I even remember moving with them to different apartments while his parents were going through their divorce and his mom asking me about birth control and pregnancy prevention, as if I was her child. My mom would come to visit me during the day on either Saturday or Sunday. Basically, I unofficially lived with them. I never fully understood why my mom agreed to let me stay with my boyfriend, but I didn't ask any questions.

As senior year progressed, my boyfriend and I began to grow a part and we finally broke up. My mom was never fond of him due to his race and where his future was heading. After harping on him for most of the two-year relationship, I finally gave in to her wishes and ended it. I recovered from the heartbreak and met another great guy, Rob, right before graduation. (This man is now my current husband.)

I had embarked on a journey to find someone who mirrored my values and aspirations. As I navigated dating and sought the right partner for a lasting marriage — considering it was my third attempt — I realized the key was finding someone who shared the same fundamental goals in life. While interests might differ, a shared commitment to personal growth and putting in the necessary effort to be better individuals was paramount. That person was Rob, even though I didn't know the full extent of his impact in my life and wouldn't learn it until much later.

"Why do you go away? So that you can come back. So that you can see the place you came from with new eyes and extra colors. And the people there see you differently, too."

— Terry Pratchett, A Hat Full of Sky

7.

Bound for Tuskegee

The decision for me to go away to college at Tuskegee was heavily influenced by family dynamics. My preference would have been to stay close to Rob and attend a college that was near enough for us to see each other with some degree of regularity. But as usual, my mom had different plans. She insisted I attend Tuskegee University, where my sister was attending school. It was my sister's dream to attend Tuskegee when we lived in Atlanta and that is exactly what she did. My mom had some wild notion that my sister would actually look out for me, even though my relationship with my sister was strained and had been for years. Never mind our combative history or the fact that she and I share no common interests. Screw the fact that my sister just didn't like me.

No matter how much I opposed her, the pressure from my mother to attend Tuskegee forced me away from other potential opportunities for nursing at East Carolina or North Carolina Central. I pondered her stubbornness for weeks and begged her to reconsider while there was still a chance to accept the offers from one of the other schools. But my mother had her say and forced me to go to Tuskegee. There was no care for how I felt about it or how I had my own, solid dreams and desires for my life. Who cares about whether my dreams were very different from my sister. Unfortunately, my mother's subtle prejudice played a significant role in her decision to push me to attend Tuskegee too. She thought because I had a Caucasian boyfriend in high school that it automatically meant that I didn't want to live or acknowledge my own race of being African American. I'm not sure what world I could ever live in that would allow me to forget that I'm Black, but her feelings were strong enough and I had no say.

Despite the challenges and disappointments, Rob and I remained great friends, despite my mother's intention to wreck our friendship. Still, I was heartbroken to be so far away from Rob on top of not getting to choose my own college.

My mom's concerns about proximity and her fantasy about my sister and I being there together, taking care of each other, took all the joy out of taking this next step in life.

But the rhythm of my life ended when I graduated. High school days were over and I landed at Tuskegee from 2000 to 2004 for undergrad and my subsequent two years of grad school from 2004 to 2006.

Now don't get me wrong, attending Tuskegee University was one of the greatest experiences of my life. HBCU love is real and it runs deep in my blood because of my instrumental experience there, but I have to be honest about how I ended up there and Tuskegee was *not* my interest nor my choice. I thought the child got to choose the college they wanted to attend, but that was only my sister's experience. Lucky her.

In August of 2000, the day arrived that I had to take the long, 12-hour road trip from DC to Tuskegee, Alabama with my mom. Luckily Rob was able to take the trip as well and he rode with us to drop me off at college. On the way there, I decided it was a good time to come clean about things. First, there was an undercurrent of distrust between my mom and me.

During the road trip, I talked to her about it, telling her that every party I went to was just that — a party. I was always where I said I was. I confessed the details about how much I drank and how we got alcohol, the crazy things we did, and the fact that I was pretty much drunk most of high school.

Let's keep it real... heavy drinking was an understatement, especially being 5'2 and 110lbs. Taking multiple shots along with my friends was a common occurrence. She never knew because, surprisingly, I could handle my liquor well enough that, even after downing a dozen shots, I could still get up and ask, "Where's the party at? Turn up the music!"

But truthfully, I was beyond ready to be an adult. I was ready to make my own decisions about how often I hung out and when I had to be home. I longed for the autonomy for all aspects of life...a piece of freedom that I still enjoy to this day. Although college was far away from everything that was familiar, I was ready to be in charge of my daily life.

Despite living within walking distance of my sister throughout college, she never took me under her wing and showed me the ropes of undergrad. 90% of the students I knew never had any idea I had a sibling, let alone one that was attending the same college.

I had spent two decades enduring her silence and waiting for her to speak, only for her voice she gained to be colder than the silence. All of the feelings I felt from her silence were confirmed in her newfound conversation. Her conversations with me were laced with criticism and judgement. She was demeaning and condescending, showing her disgust about my decision making, career moves, and how I lived my life no matter how many responsibilities I managed successfully. There were so few moments that I ever had the comfort that I was a welcomed sibling, which contributed to the growth of the tough, leathery exterior that shapes who I am today.

After years of having a sibling, I was just as out of the loop on who she is as a person as a stranger would be. That demeanor persisted until a family trip to Amsterdam that a remarkable transformation occurred — there, against the vibrant backdrop of a new environment, she discovered her voice. The city's allure seemed to awaken something within her, ultimately offering an escape big enough for the emergence of a silent voice that I once knew.

We were happy to see her breakthrough and our relationship appeared to be better on the surface. But what time revealed was a laundry list of negative views of me as a person that I never understood their origin. Our sisterhood was destined to be divided by a concrete wall between us, higher and stronger than her silence could have ever built.

"It's not the load that breaks you down; it's the way you carry it."

—Lena Horne

8.

This is Reality

I enjoyed college from an academic standpoint and I made several friendships that are still alive and thriving to this day. I found Tuskegee to be beyond challenging and now that I've survived, looking back, I did enjoy stretching my brain. Of course, what I expected about my sister "paving the way" for me turned out to be true. We spent minimal to no time together. My sister showed little interest in wanting to spend time with me, and during my freshman year, I could have used her companionship. I really needed her to take me under her wing and introduce me to her network and hang out so we'd finally build a bond. Isn't that what it's like to have an older sister? I wanted that automatic, built in friendship like I saw my friends have because she was my sister. After all of these years, I still longed for my sister to be a real sister. As you see, baggage is real.

My first year in Tuskegee was a difficult transition socially. I went from built in friendships from playing sports and partying with a strong friend group in high school to living in a place where women were brutal, cold, and just downright mean. I knew absolutely no one and found it almost impossible to make new connections with people, especially with Tuskegee having a female to male ratio of 22:1. So you can do the math on how much feminine competition existed. The absence of friends almost led me to leave Tuskegee after my first semester. It was that horrible.

In the rare times I saw my sister during the semester, it was because my mom forced the interactions or my mom gave us spending money that she needed to give me my half. Only the first few road trips home at the semester's end were done with my sister because I was never allowed to drive, we barely made conversation the entire trip, and I was forever going to be treated like the younger sister she hated. So, I rode home with my BFF Tasha, which was awesome because we could talk the day away, shared driving, and we got to be our regular, silly selves. No matter how much time went by, I was never able to pinpoint what the tuning point was in my relationship with my sister. Maybe I was too young to remember what I did, but I have no recollection of an incident or a moment. It was just one day she hated me and it stuck.

In the rare times I saw my sister, she mostly ignored me. She never particularly liked me throughout childhood, influenced by the negative image my mom has painted of me over the years, portraying me as a troublesome individual.

One day, during my first year of graduate school at Tuskegee, my phone began ringing off the hook at 1:00 am. It was my mom. I was half sleep and finally answered the phone. My mom had a stern, seriousness to her voice, which I was not expecting. She expressed that my sister was hysterically crying in the parking lot and that I needed to go and console her. I almost didn't believe her because in my entire life, I can count on one hand the amount of times I've seen my sister cry.

I was disoriented because it was the middle of the night. I couldn't understand why my mom would want me to console my sister when we all knew she didn't like me, nor would she feel comfortable speaking with me. My sister wasn't going to share a horrible, personal moment with someone she didn't trust. In fact. I was probably the last person she wanted to see. Then it hit me; why the hell is she even crying?

"Ummmmm, now why is she hysterically crying in the parking lot?" I asked my mom.

"Your dad called her." she exclaimed!

At that point, I tried to do anything I could to get off the phone and go back to sleep because there was no point in going.

"Okay and what did he say that was so upsetting?" I asked further.

My questions frustrated my mom and we were just short of arguing back and forth about why I needed to just go. I relented. We got off of the phone, I grudgingly got dressed, and I drove to where she was studying with her classmates. Her eyes were puffy from crying and there were still tears on her face. Imagine trying to console someone that you barely know despite her being your sister. She was, in reality, someone who I didn't even know had emotions at all. After probing and attempting to calm my sister, I didn't receive much information.

I left my sister to head home, trying to parse through the limited explanation she gave. The only details I received were that my dad called and that he tried to blame my mom for why we didn't see him. I was shocked that after all of these years she had this reaction to his words.

I said to myself, "My dad wouldn't have the audacity to call my cell phone. I am positive that the conversation would have been managed much differently." To this day, this incident was never spoke of again.

Despite my relationship with my sister remaining the same, other aspects of my life changed for the better. After being out of the house and some time had passed for growth, my relationship began to improve with my mom. Our conversations changed from her forcing decisions on me to allowing me the autonomy to make my own decisions. Real growth and transition. Our relationship had evolved past a tumultuous mother-daughter dynamic to a genuine friendship. Though my memories of pain and trauma revolve largely around my mother, I knew that her start in life was not easy and having children to raise on her own only exacerbated her difficulties. My dad's absence meant that my mother had to assume both parental roles, becoming both a father and a mother to my sister and me.

I always watched my mother in amazement at her strength and I developed a sincere compassion for her because of all she had been through. I know there is an inner turmoil raging within her. Like so many people, she puts on a brave face and soldiers on, silently carrying the burden of her pain. However, that never kept her from sacrificing as needed for my sister and I along the way.

My mom always warned me that other people in this life would come and go, but she was always going to be here for me no matter what happened. I believed her and watched her unwavering support. By the time I completed graduate school, my mom was one of my best friends. We talked on the phone every day. Literally — every single day, even if there was nothing to discuss. We really created an unbreakable bond that made other families jealous, as they watched us in admiration. Our conversations were real, memorable, and something that became the excitement of my car ride to work or on Saturday morning after breakfast.

My mom was my life!

"You will never know how far you can go by staying where you are."

~Unknown

9.

The Breakdown

Something broke in my relationship with my mother. And, as I noted earlier, not all broken things can be repaired. When the rift occurred, it opened fissures that had only been shoddily maintained over the years. The crack split open and the foundation under me completely crumbled.

We had to face the truth — a truth about myself, my mother, and our relationship, which opened Pandora's box so that many more truths came spilling out.

Truth is a powerful force. Some people face it with joy. Others recoil at it. And some people fight it with all their might because no one ever told them that you can't beat truth. You can deny it or accept it. But truth remains undefeated.

It was bad enough that my mother knew about the baby when she wasn't supposed to. She intruded into a space that I had reserved for my husband and me for a few weeks. But she took it one step further and decided to inform my sister, despite our explicit instructions for her to keep it private. The revelation felt like an invasion of our chosen path and the memories we were building around the pregnancy.

Following the revelation, a strange air lingered in the aftermath. My mother's behavior took an immediate, unusual turn for the worse over the following seven months. Amid this inner and family turmoil, I decided to share the news of my pregnancy with my sister after the high-risk period. I felt family harmony was more important than anything Rob and I had in mind about sharing this secret.

I contacted my sister and let her know the good news. Instead of offering congratulations or asking about my well-being (or the baby's for that matter), she questioned why I hadn't felt comfortable confiding in her earlier. The lack of enthusiasm in her response revealed a deep-seated hurt she had been carrying for years and years.

Tensions escalated as my mother expressed anger over my accusation that she purposely informed my sister before I was ready—a suspicion that ultimately proved itself to be true. In addition to the fact that Heaven and I weren't particularly close, my mother and I had candidly discussed Heaven's challenging, selfish, and mean behavior over the years.

Rob, sensing the need to clarify the situation, joined a call with my mother and me. It happened at a time when I was on bed rest due to experiencing early contractions. We just wanted to clear the air and get everyone on the same page. It was time to focus on what mattered: the new baby about to be born.

But my mother was inconsolable, her thoughts fixed on her own needs and her own anger. Despite his steadfast support and care for me during my pregnancy, she dismissed him. She didn't appreciate the way he attended to practical matters like food, groceries, dogs, and household chores. Instead, she demanded lengthy conversations with me while attempting to isolate Rob from our interactions. The strained dynamics intensified, creating a challenging environment that tested the limits of understanding and compassion within our familial bonds.

Despite my mother and I's continued daily conversations, an undeniable tension was always present in our interactions. Rob, sensing the strain getting worse in our relationship, he even took it upon himself to call my mother independently. He hoped he could be the peacemaker.

He started by acknowledging that something was amiss. The dynamics between the three of us had changed. There was an undeniable shadow over what I believed was once a close and supportive connection.

Rob, to his credit, was trying to keep the relationship from falling apart. "You have a grandchild who needs you," he pleaded with her when she started to grow distant and pulled back from us.

She answered, "I don't even care about that grandchild."

Faced with a conversation that seemed to be leading nowhere, Rob reached a point of surrender. The dialogue had become unproductive, filled with extreme and hurtful statements that could never be successfully retracted. Recognizing the futility of continuing down that path, he chose to disengage, acknowledging the detrimental nature of her behavior and the toll it was taking on all involved. It was a moment of realization that some discussions, fueled by extreme emotions and hurtful words, may be better left unresolved.

But my mother wasn't done unloading on him or me. In a bewildering turn of events, my mother began dredging up stories from my high school days, pointing out my past behavior and casting herself as the victim to my shitstorm. She described me in the most unflattering terms, as if I was a person with a vendetta. It was a strange and unexpected detour from the current situation because she was my best friend. It was a leap back in time that seemed entirely unrelated to the present circumstances nor were they memories that I could recall between us. Some were scenarios that she told me that Heaven did, but now it was changed to my name. I was her villain. Her focus on historical grievances from my high school days when I was a married woman about to have a child added a layer of confusion to the already strained dynamic.

She was coming apart at the seams and I had no idea why..

"There is hope, even when your brain tells you there isn't."

—John Green

10.

Family Dynamics

Prior to the onset of COVID, the rhythm of my life revolved around my family and it was this way for years. We were a close-knit unit, engaging in social activities and frequent travels as a collective. This was our modus operandi. My mother and sister, with relatively few friends outside the family circle, found companionship with Rob and me. We were close – not just family, but friends, navigating life together and finding comfort in each other.

During the COVID-19 pandemic, I found myself feeling as though I were in a vacuum, isolated within a bubble that distanced me from my loved ones. Many people experienced turmoil in their relationships during this challenging time, and for me, it manifested as an unexpected loss of the bond between my mother and me. The closeness I had once taken for granted with her slipped away, leaving me to grapple with an unforeseen sense of emptiness and disconnection.

But the truth of the matter is that we were already at a distance; I just didn't know it. You know how it's difficult to see how fast a baby is growing because you live with them every day. This was similar. I didn't realize things were questionable with my mother because I spoke with her every day and things seemed like the same old same old. The pandemic exposed the fragility of my relationship with my mom, and the fabric of our connection tore in two. A pandemic that initially started as three weeks turned into months and months of our lives being flipped upside down indefinitely. The everyday rat race came to a screeching halt and everything was at a standstill.

It was weird because, before COVID, people were aways hoping for a lifestyle where they could spend more time at home with their families and not work as hard. Then, when COVID forced them to do just that, it sent our society off the cliff.

Looking back, I even began to see various changes in behaviors from my mom during COVID that were starting to concern me. Honestly, even before the onset of COVID I found myself grappling with certain behaviors my mom was exhibiting. However, it was during the pandemic that the extent of her struggles came to the forefront. I could no longer deny the little hints of issues with her that surfaced from time to time throughout my childhood. Tentacles of her mental illness would come to the surface temporarily before diving back down into the abyss of her psyche.

My mom had a long history of taking anxiety medications to manage her daily moods of anxiety and depression. There was also an additional medication or two that were for the onset of a panic attack or anxiety spike. Randomly about 7 months prior to the pandemic, my mom decided that she was tired of taking her anxiety medications and she was ready to stop taking them. Keep in mind that this was not a decision that was made with a licensed professional or as a result of progress made with counseling. I had a concern, but I didn't say anything to avoid an argument or to ensure that I didn't make her feel that she was being judged. The combination of stopping her medications and the unique circumstances of the pandemic introduced an element of unpredictability to her mood, attitude, and well-being.

The absence of a supportive inner circle left her vulnerable, making most of these connections predatory in nature. She encountered a man through online dating who tried to scam her out of money and another man whose mother's murder was on unsolved mysteries. Another moment that sparked concern, but no one else fully knew the extent of her online dating experiences. Her defensiveness to my online advice made me keep my concerns to myself to ensure I kept the peace.

My mom was never one to have many friendships and the ones she had always ended for one reason or another. Jealousy, untrustworthy or just downright inconsiderate of my mother. A new friend she met in her neighborhood was another peculiar situation. He was a younger gay male around my age (30s to 40s) that she enjoyed talking to regularly. However, he was never nice to my mom and used to show her signs that he didn't care about her or her feelings. Yet, after she would complain about his behavior and I would defend her, she started getting angry with me for agreeing and saying he wasn't a good friend to her. Completely disheartening.

By the time I was seven months pregnant, she had sunk so deep into toxicity, it spread to anyone who knew and loved me like a cancer. She started behaving strangely toward my friends who had been part of our lives for years.

A long-term friend and prior co-worker, Naomi, had enjoyed a pleasant relationship with my mom, then suddenly became a target of her odd choices. For some strange reason, my mother had given Naomi's name to a prospective employer as a job recommendation, but didn't bother to tell Naomi. When Naomi told me what happened, the call from the employer she was unprepared for; of course, I was shocked and annoyed.

So, I called my mother and told her that what she did wasn't cool. In retaliation against me, my mother called Naomi complaining about the person I had become and how our relationship had changed. She spoke so horribly of me and how much of a problem I've always been. Sigh. What stuck out to me was my mom saying, "Stephanie has always been my problem child." She shared private family moments in attempt to discredit me. Then right behind this, she ended up hating Naomi because she told me these things my mom said to her "in confidence." But the only reason my mom knew Naomi was because she was my friend and we'd worked together at multiple companies.

I found it so strange that I even had to explain to my mother why this was an inappropriate thing to do. And then after the incident and my mom was gone, my husband finally shared with me the truth about the individual conversation he had with my mom. A month or so after we told my mom I was pregnant and my mom's behavior was becoming unbearable, Rob called my mom to see if he could smooth things over. He asked what could be done to improve the situation, especially considering her grandson would be arriving soon and we needed her. Her response was unhinged.

"I don't want anything to do with Stephanie because this is who she's always going to be. Stephanie's always been a problem; she holds on to things and won't let them go. I'm done with Stephanie."

I can't even express how crushing this was to hear. Literally, there was nothing that I could have done to prevent this situation because she was done with me and I just had no idea. What kind of person would talk to someone every day, multiple times per day, for over 15 years if they were done with you? And then to hear how I've been painted as this horrible person despite priding myself on being honest and my willingness to give the shirt off of my back to my family. Over 15 years of what I thought was having the strongest mother-daughter bond that ever existed was diminished down to nothing. In some regards my mother was right, I didn't let things go because they kept happening.

My mom and my sister both exhibited consistent, horrific behavior that was cyclical. I'd express how I didn't like what they did (unsupportiveness, mean comments, gaslighting), they'd apologize and then do it again, so of course I have to bring it up again. Let's be clear, issues were rarely discussed in my family, so these occurrences of confrontation were few and far between despite how often they happened. Then to hear that she was done with me, months before my letter to her in August; this outcome was going to happen no matter what I did. I thought we were BFFs that could find common ground and my mom was committed to hating me. Why?

Any time I received lump sums of money from work or taxes, I always gave my mom a certain percentage for her to pay off bills, to get ahead, and to give her a small financial break if I could, for all she had done for me. Right before and during the pandemic, she began lying about where she was spending her money. Somehow she ended up with a $5000 line of credit from Home Depot for home improvements. I remember explaining over and over that she had to pay off the balance in 6 months to avoid the interest, but she was bewildered. She mentioned an $1100 medical bill from her ongoing breast cancer maintenance, so I gave her $1500 when I received my next bonus. Instead of paying the medical bill, she bought an electric bike for $900. My mom wanted the electric bike for exercise. I know that sounds strange because it sounded strange to me. I knew she wanted to get out of the house since the pandemic was isolating, but an electric bike will never be a real source of exercise because it has a motor. But, once again I kept my thoughts to myself because I didn't want her to feel attacked.

There were even a few times that my mother fell and hurt herself. One fall was after COVID and she slipped on some ice and hurt her wrist. Her wrist was hurt for months following that fall and I never could get my sister to understand my concern. I did my best to express my concern about our mom falling and not being able to control the 2 large dogs she has, but I was always ignored. I was always viewed as being dramatic over something that wasn't that serious. My mother is in her 60s and she is at a higher risk of injury from falls. I never understood why my concerns were ignored, but it fueled me to keep my mouth shut even when I should have spoken up.

Months into COVID, my mother's reckless and unpredictable behavior continued. My mom and my sister were both tyrants to Rob and I about following quarantine rules; yet they both were going out to eat at restaurants and my mom attended Black Lives Matter rallies and protests. It was perplexing that they kept such a short leash on me, but neither of them stayed as close to home the way my husband and I did.

Four years later. I found an old email to my mother that was written almost a year into the pandemic, discussing how her moods and behaviors were disheartening and I didn't know how to help her.

Regrettably, my mother seemed unaware that she needed to learn and evolve to adapt to the changing circumstances. Life was throwing her some serious curveballs that she never learned to field. This lack of adjustment and inability to pivot resulted in her experiencing the consequences that often befall those who resist transformation. It's a reminder of the importance of growth and adaptation that are needed in the face of life's challenges.

She grew bitter over time. I watched her mental state spiral out until she was no longer able to hold the family together and, in some ways, helped to tear it apart. This is why I call this period "The COVID Chronicles." COVID was the tipping point, a moment in time that can never be reversed and has the potential to change everything that happens next.

A lot of people went through something similar, where their lives were seemingly fine before COVID, but the events of the crisis brought out something in them or their inner circle they didn't know was there. Years later, they find themselves still trying to figure out what the hell happened and how to put the pieces back together. Being alone like my mother really had a profound impact on her. The isolation might have spared us the virus, but it cost us all a piece of our sanity.

I also know that nothing is coincidental. So, what occurred had to happen for a reason. It was a forced and fast evolution for every living human being. People around the world were spending more time alone. There was more time for introspection which many of us hadn't done in years — or ever. We were moving so fast before COVID slowed us down, we didn't have time to think about our lives and our relationships. COVID forced us to sit still and be more contemplative. There was so much brewing that didn't come to light until we hit the brakes on life.

Despite my mother's longstanding wish for a close-knit family, her actions seemed to dismantle the very bond she said she wanted. I realized that the mother I wanted was worlds away from the one I had.

"I'm not upset that you lied to me, I'm upset that, from now on, I can't believe you."

— Friedrich Nietzsche

11.

Seeking Closure

I had an epiphany that I needed my parents' divorce papers to find out the truth versus relying on someone's version of the story. I started my search online and kept running into roadblocks. I didn't have much of the information I needed to get the answers. I didn't know the date of their marriage or divorce. I didn't have a case number or the type of case. And every search of my parents' names alone kept coming back empty. I was frustrated beyond belief. But I've learned that you sometimes have to walk away from a problem for a moment and come back with fresh eyes and a clear mind.

I waited two weeks and tried again. This time, it occurred to me that the years I lived in San Diego might serve as a lead. It did. Within two minutes of searching, case number connected to my maiden name within the years I searched and I was on my way.

My parents divorced when I was four. The divorce papers answered that question for me. The terms of the divorce were a matter of public record. The San Diego court papers classified their case as "Dissolution with Minor Children."

I had been told by my mother that the marriage ended because my father was a lay about and she was doing all the work to support the children. In addition, she said he left because he didn't want any more children. I was fed these stories. But my mother was the petitioner. It would seem that, if my dad wanted out, he would be the petitioner.

I continued to dig for information by calling my mother's friend. She told me that the story of my mother's daycare was not complete. My mother had always credited this friend as the one who helped her start her daycare. But the friend said it was my dad who poured time and money into getting the daycare going, not her. What's worse is that my mother broke off their friendship abruptly after years of our families being together. She knew that my mother was angry with her about something but had no idea what. They had been on a trip to Salt Lake City. Something upset my mother and she didn't speak to her friend for the entire 14-hour ride back, never sharing with her friend what upset her.

This was her pattern. My mom's trust issues pushed me away, pushed Rob away, and countless others. She even pushed her sisters away. I later learned that one of her sister's tried to convince her to reconcile with me, to address my feelings, and take her place as a grandmother. She wouldn't… or couldn't. Sigh.

Although I am enduring the pain that comes with sensitive investigations, I had to know the complete truth. The online documents were incomplete and I needed to get to San Diego. But first, I had a few more people to talk to.

I had a conversation with my ex-boyfriend's mother from High School to gain some clarity on the extended periods of time when I didn't even live with my mom.

"Your mom kind of abandoned you. She didn't leave money for you either, so I paid for all of your needs because you were my kid. I loved you as if you were my own." she stated.

Apparently, my mom would come to pick me up on Saturdays for the day. Almost like visitation for child support. Then it was back to my school schedule with my boyfriend's family.

She finally came back to get me and for me to come with her. The only caveat was that she had found a house in a new school district that was a poorly performing one. She had promised me, after all the moving around we had done, that I would not have to change schools again. But here we were planning to move once again, making me the "new" kid.

"Do you want to move with me into the new house or stay here?" my mom asked.

Of course, I loved school and my friends, so I told her no; I wanted to stay where I was, like she promised. Then another epiphany occurred, that this was the high school situation my mom kept referring to that I never understood. She wanted me to pick her and this was her example where she could classify me as constantly choosing others over her. She couldn't understand that I was choosing my life, the life I fought to build.

Another conversation I had was with my mom's ex-boyfriend, Maleek, because he was around when I graduated high school and went off to college. Apparently, Maleek put pressure on my mom to go get me and bring me home to the new home she had purchased. So, did my mom come get me because of a genuine love or longing for me or to put on the act to win this relationship with Maleek? I'll never know if it was genuine or not.

Then I asked my last question, "Why did you and my mother break up?"

I was always told that they broke up because he wanted to have more kids, which she was unable to give him, but that wasn't true. Maleek and my sister had an unbearable, contentious relationship. Despite the fact that she was painfully quiet, she found her voice when it came to Maleek. She was combative verbally with him to the point that he chose to stop dating my mother.

Have gratitude for the things you're discarding. By giving gratitude, you're giving closure to the relationship with that object, and by doing so, it becomes a lot easier to let go.

—Marie Kondo

12.

Finding My Father

The story of my father's true whereabouts and where he had been all my childhood was starting to unfold. And it was casting my mother in an ugly light. Not only had she lied about who he was and what happened to him, she stood in the way of our relationship for 40 years.

It started when I ended my relationship with my mother. Her mental illness had grown out of control, and I wouldn't subject myself, Rob, or our baby to it. But, as I pondered her strange behavior, I started to call into question everything she told me — especially the stories she told me about my father.

I decided to investigate to see if I could verify anything she said. As I did, I learned more and more. I reached out to others in my parents' story who knew them back when they were first together. Some were willing to share all they knew. Others, like my mom's ex-fiancée, wouldn't call me back.

I knew that I had a half-brother, my father's son with another woman, but we never had a relationship.

My counselor had encouraged me to call him a year earlier after I learned that he kept in touch with my father. Their relationship was strained, but I knew they stayed in communication. Looking back, I wish I had taken her advice earlier. I might have spared myself a lot of heartache I experienced over that year as my relationship with my mother disintegrated.

There was also a half-sister who was someone I wanted to get to know. They were both my siblings, and I didn't appreciate being denied the chance to meet them. This was real life. We didn't grow up in the same household. It wasn't a picturesque family. But I wanted to have a shot at a relationship with them. I didn't feel I had the freedom to reach out to them before because I didn't want to risk offending my mother or sister. But with the two of them out of the way, I was free to follow my heart.

My brother was open to the conversation and even agreed to get my sister in touch with me. He mentioned that my father had lived with my sister for a while to help her take care of her kids. When I spoke with her, she had only good things to say about him. He was not the monster my mother claimed to have to keep me away from.

After interviewing everyone I could, I realized that much of what I thought I knew about my parents was not true. I would need documentation to bring this story full circle and fill in the blanks in the story. The only to do that was to go to San Diego where my parents lived when they were married.

It was a bold move, but Rob supported me every step of the way. I set off San Diego to visit the courthouse and see if I could get my hands on my parents' divorce papers, knowing that the divorce papers would show the details of their life. Maybe there would be some clues to fill the gaps in my childhood. I wanted all the records: vehicles owned, homes purchased, assets they shared, debts they acquired as well as information about me, other children, ages, birthdays, etc. And I knew the divorce papers would reveal one critical piece of information: the name of the petitioner – the person filing for the divorce. It's all documented. And the questions of whether my mother lied when she said that my father abandoned me would surely be answered.

I felt I couldn't trust anything she said about my early years. My mother painted my father as a deadbeat, but the papers would be the final arbiter, revealing whether he was in arrears on child support too. Lastly, I would learn about their custody arrangement, as the papers would explain why the children were in the custody of one parent and not the other.

We rushed off to San Diego. I had to do this because I was dealing with my mother whose mental health issues may have caused her to hide the truth from me.

My husband went through this entire process with me, sharing the burden of each shock in lockstep. We sat on the plane, holding hands, and preparing ourselves for anything.

We weren't just finding out who my father was. We were learning who my mother was and who I was at the same time. This was a monumental moment.

There were always things that didn't make sense about my backstory, but I was too young to decipher it all and too focused on survival to care. But now that Rob and I were stabilized in our lives and happily married, it was time to get to the truth. With actual papers, not hearsay, we would be able to piece the story together.

Best of all, thanks to my half-siblings, my father agreed to call me.

Hope is like the sun, which, as we journey toward it, casts the shadow of our burden behind us.

—Samuel Smiles

13.

My Father's Voice.

At the age of 40, I finally got to talk to him.

I waited by the phone to see if I would hear from my father. My dad called 30 minutes later after speaking with my half-sister. It was hard to even know where to begin a conversation. We hadn't talked once in 34 years. But we had an instant connection as we poured over the experiences both he and I had with my mom. It was like he could finish my sentences.

He described my mother as someone who wasn't able to accept people for who they really are. I could relate since much of my life centered around her disapproval of me as a person. She and my sister didn't accept me at all. In the same breath, he never spoke negative of her and always hoped that she would trust him one day.

He expressed that she was the only woman he ever loved.

He said there was a time when my sister was in vet school and he called to establish a connection with her. I remembered my sister revealing that he had called her. But I never knew what was said between them. What I did know what they my mother called me in the middle of the night to tell me that I should console Heaven because our Dad had called her. I rushed to my sister's side to console her even though I didn't know why. Finally, I asked what he said that was so upsetting. She said that he had blamed the separation on my mom.

What I found out — what my father shared — was that both he and my mother were at fault. He was honest about his role but wasn't about to let my mother refuse to share the blame. The reason I was given for why he left was actually not true. He didn't leave; my mother left him.. And he was never living off the grid. In fact, he was working as an engineer for years and then moved to LA with my half-sister..

He always had a job in Las Vegas that was legitimate. My father's whereabouts were always known to her. She could have reached him at any time. All of the graduation cards to my grandmother were just a rouse to sell the act.

What happened was that, during their marriage, my mother claimed that she needed to move to a warmer place because my sister and I were sickly with constant ear infections. No one knows to this day if that's true. But my mother convinced my dad to move us away from the cold weather on the east coast to a warm climate. He dropped out of school and quit his job so they could move back to San Diego. They moved into a house he already owned, and he put my mother on the deed.

My dad helped my mom start a daycare business she claimed she wanted to run. He wanted to get away from contract work and start his own contracting business. But my mother didn't want him to do it and convinced him to stay with the corporate jobs he was getting. She felt those jobs were more reliable.

They were doing well at that point, making a lot of money. They were the Joneses people wanted to keep up with.

My mother decided at some point that she didn't want to run a daycare and, in fact, shouldn't have to work at all. She had always wanted to be a kept woman, staying home. She issued an ultimatum to my father that if she couldn't, she would divorce him.

My mother had severe trust issues according to my dad. It didn't matter how much he did. She was never satisfied. I knew what he meant as I felt the same in my relationship with her. Whatever her personal traumas were, my mother never fully learned to trust people in her life.

These stories gave me perspective and filled in the gaps. What he said made sense, and I knew that my dad's stories and my mom's couldn't both be true. At first, I felt relieved. But the truth was that I needed to confirm which version of my history was true.

What I needed was documentation.

I'm going in. I'm gonna invest in everything that I want... to make life be exactly what I want.

—Trina

14.

Documentation

Walking into the courthouse presented a mix of emotions. I felt strangely empowered but nervous at the same time. All kinds of memories flooded my mind as I walked down the hall. There was no turning back now.

With case numbers in hand, I was determined to get this documentation.

Curiously, when I arrived at the courthouse, the clerk directed me to a printer and instructed me to log in the case number and send any documents to the printer that I needed copies of. The first file I saw was just two pages long. I was so disappointed; but I saw that it was just a summary of the processing of their paperwork. I look back at the clerk and come to find out, I was at the wrong computer. Finally at the right computer, I input the case number and the actual divorce document appeared. The first thing I noticed was the size of the divorce file. My divorce was a little over a dozen pages long. Most people I talked to said theirs were similar. My parents' divorce document? It was 306 pages long. And, to add to my shock, there was a second divorce decree from another marriage. It cost me over $150 just to print the documentation.

My jaw dropped. Did I really have the document? Yes, I had the documentation.

With documents in hand, I rushed back to the hotel. As soon as I got into the hotel room, my husband and I read through every single page and read every line. Over the next few weeks, we constructed a timeline to be sure we had the entire story to explain what took place.

Here's what we learned:

My parents were married just shy of nine years and had gotten pregnant with my sister about three months after they were married. It took nearly four years for the divorce to be finalized.

The house my family lived in was originally my father's house. He added her to the deed in a bid to quiet her mistrust. My dad wanted to prove that he was in the marriage for the long haul and the best way to do that was to add her to the deed as soon as they moved back to San Diego.

In the divorce, she decided to repay his kindness by trying to take his house away right from under him..

As I mentioned, he helped her start her daycare business and they were doing well financially, earning what would equate to a six-figure income today. But, when she closed the daycare, she then left my dad and filed for welfare benefits. I was in shock that we fell so far.

The divorce was filed when I was four. My father was served June 5th at our home. I got the feeling that my dad had no idea that my mother was considering divorce because he was served at home. The divorce included:

- A restraining order to stay at least 100 feet away
- A no-contact order
- Property restraint
- Child support request of $350 per child per month.
- Spousal support request
- Attorney's fees.

The question of why it was difficult to see my dad was answered. Since he dropped out of school and left his job in upstate New York to move back to San Diego, he was in the very early stages of building his own business. He had to workday and night to pay a lawyer to defend himself. Had he followed his dream of leaving his government contract jobs and started his own business, he might have been in a better financial position, working for himself. He wanted the same dream of entrepreneurship as my mother.

Two weeks later, she extended the temporary restraining order to keep him away. In July, she agrees to joint physical custody. Of course, he couldn't come to our home when there was a standing restraining order against him threatening arrest if he showed up at the home. How could he share custody with a restraining order?

My mother hired a high-priced lawyer, who was suggested by my grandmother. Then, my father moved out with no place to go. Shockingly, I actually remember the day he left. Then he was ordered to pay child support at a time when he had no job or a place to live.

Essentially, my mother made it impossible for me to spend time with my father. In February of 1988, my sister and I were psychologically evaluated as a result of Child Protective Services getting involved with our family. Their recommendation was that we should stay in the family home to maintain continuity for us kids. We don't know who contacted CPS, but I had started a habit of stealing that was mentioned in the evaluation... maybe it was because of that.

My mother started dating as soon as my father left and I even caught her having sex with one of the guys in our home. Then she moved us in with her boyfriend. June of 1988, she insisted that the divorce settle quickly so she could marry her new man.

Later that month, my dad was arrested for lack of payment of child support and lack of responsiveness to court orders. My father was thrown in jail. My mother instructed him to go back to the contract work similar to his role in NY he had before. It seemed as if she was orchestrating his return to that job so ultimately she could benefit. Plus, throughout the divorce documents, she continued to press my dad to give her the house and he continued to refuse.

April of 1990, my mother took out a home equity loan of $40,000 on the house my father bought. She was approved, but not with the permission of my father or her lawyer. There's a statement from the lawyer that even he wasn't unaware of the home equity loan because my mother mentioned getting a personal loan. A few months later, my mother got married to a man named Milton who came to live with us.

After almost 3 years of continued court litigation from my mother, my mom was finally awarded custody and child support. The house sold immediately thereafter and my mother collected child support from him from the proceeds of the house. The child support amount was calculated in full to include back child support and child support was paid up through the age of 18 years old for my sister and me. The child support was $100 per child per month, which was lowered from $350 due to my father having minimal income being self-employed. What a bargain we were. She didn't get all the money of course because she was forced to pay back the home equity loan at the time of the sale. But what's disheartening is that my father got nothing from his own home. With his child support paid up, all he could do was continue to move on. He actually fought for custody of us within the three-year court litigation, but the courts at that time were not inclined to separate kids from their mothers.

My mother moved us with Milton to a trailer where she burned through the money she had collected from my father. Less than two years after they married, Milton divorced her after all the money was gone.

And the stories I was told? Well... they were all proven to be untrue.

My father being off the grid: untrue.

My father paying no child support: untrue.

My father abandoning me: untrue.

And, in a most cunning move, my mother filed for more child support in an attempt to double-dip, exploiting the weaknesses she saw in the child-support system. Thankfully, someone figured it out and refused to grant her more.

"What I learned in this tragedy was the eternal lesson of good people going bad."

— Steven Ramirez, Tell Me When I'm Dead

15.

No Regrets

I am all about acceptance. I want to be accepted just as I work to be accepting of others. I never received that from my mother though I have longed for it almost my whole life. I know that revealing the truth makes it harder to have her acceptance. But truth is paramount.

So, where are we today?

I love my mother more than I can express. There is no love lost. After all we've been through, one might think I don't love her. But that is not the case.

I have taken financial care of her and I've supported her in more ways than I can count. Without her, I wouldn't be here today. The person she is essentially forced me to be who I am; and I love who I am.

So, strangely I have to thank her for my life because it was because of the life she provided that I was able to have my children. Regardless of the difficulties, she played a huge role in who I am today. She's the one who taught me to be honest above all else. She taught me to take care of my friendships so I could share life with others.

That said, I was also told that there are major divides in our family that I am unable to cross. One major obstacle is religion which seems to give people ample excuse to separate themselves from others who don't believe as they do.

But this is yet another facet of my life that was shaped by my mother's narrative. She shaped our constant moves across the country by saying it was necessary for our financial improvement and because we weren't accepted by our family's religion.

There were times when our extended family came to visit us, but it was always a one-off. There was never any long-lasting connection with other family members and as a kid I never maintained relationships with my cousins. I knew that my aunt was a devoted Jehovah's witness and she would mention her faith in challenging times. My mother took it personally and viewed her professions of faith as attempts to convert her. When I spoke with my aunt, she explained that the entire family would love to reconcile with her. My mother has always expressed her desire for unconditional love, but she can't see the love that surrounds her from me, Rob, my aunt, and so many others. Overall, my investigation did not reveal any issues around religion at all.

This is the threat of undiagnosed or untreated mental illness. Its tentacles reach far into a person's life. My mother's issues reach back to her mother and potentially back farther than that. Being in relationship with her at this point means never knowing what's true and what isn't.

For that reason, we must all give each other grace and time to summon the courage to seek the help we need to be okay again.

In truth, I was so close to mom, in part, because of the absence of my father. Things were good with us at first. But she worked three jobs and the strain started to crack her already fragile mental state. She was functioning as a mom and a dad.

Her goal was for us to be together forever,— her, my sister, and me. What should have happened was that my sister's spouse and my spouse and our children should have been folded into our bond. But that didn't happen, not for any length of time. I knew that my mom struggled with depression, but the extent of her issues was hidden until she reached a breaking point.

127

Today, we are estranged. There is no contact and hasn't been since 2021. Three months before everything collapsed, I could tell my mother and sister had an issue with me, but neither of them was willing to come out with it. That's how I knew my mother had spilled the tea on my pregnancy.

The one thing my mother always wanted was a close-knit family. Sadly, it was the thing her actions consistently destroyed. And now, the burden is hers to mend what's broken.

I have had to come to the difficult point of acceptance that my mother is not the person who gave birth to me. Just a parent that must someday look at their child and acknowledge that they've become an adult, I must look at my mother and acknowledge that she has transformed into some new version of herself too.

I wish I could end this book with the happy news of reconciliation. I can't. What I can say is that the door is always open. It has to be. And for those who are reading this and thinking of their own struggles, I want to share my hope with you. Keep an open heart even if it must be a protected heart. People do change. It may take years of therapy, prescription treatments, and hard work, but humans are capable of growth. We must be there to celebrate their accomplishments when they do, knowing that, someday, we will be there to accept them again.

The blessing is that I've gotten to know my dad and gave him the chance of getting to know me. He was ripped from my life for no reason. But I have him back and we are looking toward the future together.

I know I am not the only person in the world to have experienced such trauma. My task today is trying to salvage these relationships with him, my siblings, my cousins, and others.

This is the pain of concealing the truth. It required me to embark on a mission to unearth it all. It fell like a nuclear bomb went off in my life and I am still sifting through the ash.

Do I have any regrets? No, not one.

I don't regret what I've been through. I've had ups and downs, super highs and some really low lows. I've been so blessed that I could never say, 'I wish this didn't happen.' It's part of who I am. There's nothing in my life that's an accident.

—Jennifer Lopez

CONCLUSION

I always remind myself that I am not the only person in the world to have experienced such trauma, although this experience has been a lonely one. I know that there are always others who are experiencing something similar or that they have survived the hardship. Life's negative scenarios do not happen in a vacuum and we can learn lessons and strategies to survive from others. As I reflect on my journey, I am proud of how I have navigated the complexities of mental health. Especially being African American, where we learn generational curses of suffering in silence. I've come to realize that the lessons learned along the way have been invaluable even though they were significantly painful. Each experience, whether challenging or uplifting, has contributed to my understanding of the intricate relationship between mental well-being and everyday life.

It's important to understand that mental health can have generational impacts if unaddressed. Unfortunately, I'm a product of unaddressed mental health. Leaving them to fester or compartmentalizing them forces people to withdraw to save themselves.

Here are some lessons that have profoundly shaped my perspective:

1. **Acceptance is the First Step:** Acknowledging the presence of mental health challenges is the first step towards healing and growth. Denial only perpetuates suffering, but acceptance opens the door to healing and support.

2. **Self-Compassion is Vital**: Learning to be gentle with yourself in times of struggle is crucial. Just as we would extend compassion to a friend facing difficulties, we must offer the same kindness to ourselves.

3. **Seeking Help is Strength, Not Weakness:** There is immense strength in reaching out for help when needed. It takes courage to ask for support, and doing so should be applauded, never ridiculed.

4. **Communication is Key**: Honest and open communication fosters understanding and connection. By expressing our thoughts and emotions, we invite others into our inner world, breaking down barriers and fostering empathy.

5. **Progress is Nonlinear**: Healing is not always a linear journey; it's filled with ups and downs, twists and turns. There are gains and losses. Embracing the nonlinear nature of progress allows for greater flexibility and resilience in the face of challenges as long as we don't give up.

6. **Self-Care is Essential, Not Selfish**: Prioritizing self-care is not selfish; it's a necessary act of self-preservation. Engaging in activities that nourish the mind, body, and soul replenishes our reserves, enabling us to better cope with life's demands. And stepping away from toxic relationships is wise, not cruel. You may want to later open the door to reconciliation once the issues have been addressed. That may mean counseling, medication, or other steps. Be strong during the separation. Don't cave to empty promises. Insisting that someone address

their mental health concerns is the way to help them get better.

7. **Vulnerability is a Strength:** Embracing vulnerability cultivates authenticity and deepens connections with others. By allowing ourselves to be seen, flaws and all, we invite genuine relationships grounded in trust and acceptance.

8. **Mindfulness Cultivates Presence**: Practicing mindfulness enables us to cultivate present-moment awareness and navigate life with greater clarity and intention. By anchoring ourselves in the here and now, we can more effectively manage stress and enhance overall well-being. While it's fun to imagine what can be, we can't use fantasy land as a means of ignoring reality.

9. **Empathy Fosters Connection**: Cultivating empathy towards ourselves and others helps us grow meaningful connections and fosters a sense of belonging. By stepping into another's shoes, we bridge the gap between us, fostering compassion and understanding.

10. **Hope is a Powerful Force**: In the darkest of moments, hope has the power to

illuminate the path forward. Holding onto hope, even when faced with adversity, fuels resilience and propels us towards brighter tomorrows.

These lessons have served as guiding principles throughout my journey, illuminating the path forward and reminding me of the inherent strength within. By embracing the complexities of mental health and the lessons learned along the way, I've discovered a newfound sense of authenticity.

Mental health is a topic often shrouded in misconceptions and stereotypes. When we think of mental health issues, the images that often come to mind are those of extreme cases—individuals confined to institutions, wandering aimlessly through the streets, unable to function in society, or struggling to communicate "normally." While these are certainly valid experiences within the spectrum of mental health, but they represent only a fraction of the broader reality.

In truth, mental health ranges from flourishing to struggling, and everything in between. It's not just drug addicts or alcoholics. In my case, mental illness is the inability of my mom to let things go or to control her extreme thoughts and behaviors. It's almost borderline personality disorder mixed with slight schizophrenia. Despite if I hurt her feelings, she should have been able to see the bigger picture of being a grandmother versus leaving my life. A mother leaving their kid's life is almost unheard of in our society, yet my mom and sister have left without any plans to return. It's not always visible on the surface, and many people navigate their daily lives with undiagnosed or unseen challenges. It's time to stop the suffering of people silently grappling with their mental well-being, making each breath feel like a struggle. It's the pervasive sense of emptiness and numbness that colors every interaction, leaving people feeling disconnected from the world around them.

As my understanding of mental health expands, there are also lessons learned that I must keep in the forefront of my mind as well. This incident was not my fault (exhales). I only have control of my actions. I have to let go. And I cannot concern myself with what others think. I've placed guilt on myself that is heavier than the world on your shoulders.

I fully understand that setting new boundaries and expressing my feelings is jarring and it can sting. But real, familial relationships are built on weathering worthwhile storms. Blaming myself completely negates the role my mother and sister have played. Therefore, letting go is the only way to heal. Trusting that life will give you something better than whatever it asks you to give up.

As for Rob, he continues to be the joy of my life. Every day, I recognize the value of the partnership we have, ensuring that I never take it for granted. Rob and I weathered the various stages of evolution together, experiencing the highs and lows, and witnessed each other's true selves. The transparency in our relationship, even during periods when we didn't anticipate being together, fostered a deep understanding of each other's flaws, vulnerabilities, and strengths.

I find myself willingly doing anything for Rob, a level of commitment I didn't experience in my previous marriages. Unlike those instances where I resisted change, for Rob, I'm always prepared to transform. It's not just about love; it's about believing that he genuinely cares about my well-being. In contrast to past relationships where I hesitated to change, I know that his desire for my transformation stems from a genuine wish to see me become a better person. We agree that each of us must work independently and with others to grow into the best version of ourselves we can discover. And that often means addressing past traumas, hidden hurts, and mental health concerns.

In our society, there is a stigma surrounding mental health—a belief that acknowledging struggles is a sign of weakness, and seeking help is a sign of failure. This stigma can prevent people from reaching out for support, leading them to suffer in silence and isolation.

Mental health issues touch absolutely every family. None of us are spared. And, in the years following COVID, we have all suffered a blow to our mental health and we need to take steps to take care of our minds and emotions the same we do our bodies.

It starts with each of us recognizing that mental health is a universal concern. As we work to build a more compassionate and inclusive society, we have to remember that mental health is not always the extreme version that we are taught. It can affect an everyday person that we interact with — a colleague, a friend, a family member — whose struggles may be unseen and undiagnosed. And it's up to each of us to extend a hand of empathy and support, creating a world where everyone feels seen, heard, and valued.

"I always believed that when you follow your heart or your gut, when you really follow the things that feel great to you, you can never lose, because settling is the worst feeling in the world."

—Rihanna

Epilogue

I could not close this book without a few words about the power of truth. Truth is a universal principle that transcends cultural, social, and individual boundaries. It has been a subject of philosophical, ethical, and religious contemplation throughout human history. The power of truth lies in its ability to reveal itself over time. Truth doesn't really like to be hidden and it always seems to find a way to rise to the surface When it does, it has a transformative impact on individuals and societies.

Like a hidden treasure, truth often requires our help to bring it to the surface. This book was meant to explore the significance of personal and family truth.

The passage of time and forces of nature eventually bring the concealed truth to the surface like a dead body. Attempts to bury, suppress, or distort the truth may succeed temporarily, but they are destined to fail. Ultimately, the truth is always revealed.

History is replete with examples of individuals and institutions attempting to conceal inconvenient truths. Whether in the realms of politics, science, or personal relationships, buried truths have an uncanny ability of resurfacing, often at the most unexpected moments.

On the flip side, truth is the treasure we gain if we have the courage to pursue it. Yes, it can be tough to look at it when it shines so brightly, it seems to blind us.

It's no accident that truth is often associated with light, a metaphor that underscores its ability to dispel darkness and bring clarity to obscured situations. The illumination provided by truth is not merely a physical phenomenon but extends to the realm of knowledge, understanding, and awareness.

But the reward of seeking and finding truth is having greater levels of courage, intellectual curiosity, and closure, bringing value and richness to those who dare to unearth it.

Just as treasure hunters must navigate obstacles and overcome challenges in their quest for hidden wealth, seekers of truth must confront barriers such as deception, misinformation, and vested interests. The act of uncovering truth involves digging deep into the layers of information, questioning assumptions, and challenging established narratives. In doing so, individuals not only discover the truth but also develop a deeper understanding of the complexities that surround it.

Truth is also healing. Its revelation has the potential to mend wounds, both individual and collective. When truth comes to light, it serves as a catalyst for healing, offering individuals the opportunity to confront and address the pain caused by deception or concealment.

Truth plays a pivotal role in the dynamics of forgiveness and reconciliation. The revelation of truth is often a prerequisite for genuine forgiveness, as it provides the necessary context for understanding the actions or events that led to harm or conflict. Without a clear understanding of the truth, forgiveness will be superficial, lacking the depth needed for genuine reconciliation.

Confessing truth is sometimes the only way to rebuild relationships and create a framework for coexistence. The power of truth is in its ability to serve as a foundation for trust that makes relationships feel safe. When parties involved in a conflict or dispute confront the truth together, it becomes a shared experience that can bridge divides and facilitate genuine reconciliation.

Make no mistake, however, truth comes with risks. Many people get themselves invested in the lie and will throw up barriers to the disclosure of truth. At times, the only way to get to the truth you desire, is to move those barriers aside and let everyone involved have access to the facts.

It was no easy task for me to confront the truth. But I walk in the light of day now, knowing who I am and understanding my history far better than I ever could. Yes, I suffered losses. But, for me, truth was the prize I refused to be denied.

Empower yourself by searching for the right question as if it were a buried treasure and treasures will find you.

—John Fairclough

ABOUT THE AUTHOR

Stephanie Harris is a fresh face in the world of non-fiction. Her debut memoir, "Unrealized Reality" is a gripping, candid depiction of generational curses intertwined with mental health and the crumbling of a reality that she once knew.

A San Diego native, Stephanie holds masters' degrees in Biology and Public Health, but her true lifelong love is in creating voiceover content for multiple companies across the world where she uses her passion for acting to bring commercials, promos, animation, and narration to life. She's the wife of a Physical Therapist, the mother of two toddlers, and when she takes time to relax you can find her traveling across the world, enjoying cultural traditions one country at a time.

Stephanie brings a level of raw authenticity to her writing that's both rare and emotion provoking. Stephanie believes that if you are led by fear, you may never get a chance to experience the true joy and rewards that life has to offer.

You can find more about her interests, thoughts, writing journey and future projects on her on IG @.dreamymincus

If you enjoyed this book, please take a moment to leave us a review. Reviews are the best way to ensure this story is shared with others. Thank you for your support.

Stephanie Harris